EFFECTIVE

MW01102035

Forthcoming titles in this series will include

- *Winning Sales Letters*
- *Win–Win Negotiation*
- *How to Wow and Audience*
- *Make the Most of Meetings*
- *Key Account Management*
- *Coping with Company Politics*
- *Winning CVs*
- *How to Pay Less Tax*

Do you have ideas for subjects which could be included in this exciting and innovative series? Could your company benefit from close involvement with a forthcoming title?

Please contact David Grant Publishing Limited
80 Ridgeway, Pembury, Tunbridge Wells, Kent TN2 4EZ
Tel/Fax +44 (0)1892 822886
Email GRANTPUB@aol.com
with your ideas or suggestions.

EFFECTIVE

DIRECT MAIL

John Frazer-Robinson

60 Minutes Success Skills Series

Copyright © John Frazer-Robinson 1999

First published 1999 by
David Grant Publishing Limited
80 Ridgeway
Pembury
Kent TN2 4EZ
United Kingdom
Tel/Fax +44 (0)1892 822886
Email GRANTPUB@aol.com

01   00   99   10 9 8 7 6 5 4 3 2 1

60 Minutes Success Skills Series is an imprint of
David Grant Publishing Limited

British Library Cataloguing in Publication Data
A CIP catalogue record for this book is available from the British Library

ISBN 1-901306-25-9

Cover design: Liz Rowe
Text design: Graham Rich
Production coordinator: Paul Stringer
Edited and Typeset in Futura by Kate Williams
Printed and bound in Great Britain by
T.J. International Ltd, Padstow, Cornwall

This book is printed on acid-free paper

CONTENTS

ABOUT *EFFECTIVE DIRECT MAIL*

The family of an American friend of mine owned a small business in Atlantic City, New Jersey, which became a very successful *big* business. Luckily for them, among their numbers they had one of the most talented direct mailers in the USA. He once said to me:

> **❝** *Dollar for dollar, no advertising medium will return more to your business than direct mail.* **❞**
> **– Murray Raphel, US Direct Mail Expert and Retail Business Proprietor**

Believe him!

Getting what you want

You are probably wondering if, in just 60 minutes, you can really get a good enough grasp of direct mail to become successful at it. The answer is Yes – and No.

Yes, you can pick up the basics. Yes, you can learn some vital do's and don'ts. And yes, you can use the tips and hints and invaluable checklists that you will find in this book.

Why No? Because I think you will find that it pays you to read the book quickly to start with, and it should be a great start. But as you gradually master the business of effective direct mail, you'll probably find it useful to keep the book handy.

How to get the most from this book

Take a read – guzzle it all down in one go. Then try to give yourself a little more time. The great thing about direct mail is that you'll find it well worth your time and thought. Given another read, you'll be able to set what the book says against the perspective of your own business, your own desires and intentions, and your own experience.

From then on, why not read one chapter a week and go on re-reading at that pace until you feel you've really absorbed it.

But mostly, keep it handy when you are actually getting your mailing together. Dip in to it to remind yourself and to stay fresh. Check your progress against all the checklists and tips and hints.

How to get more still from this book

If you are writing and designing a website or sending e-mailings as well as direct mailings, you'll find most of the advice in this book is just as valuable; and just as valid.

What's in this chapter for you

Think small, think close
How much can you afford to spend?
What do you want to do?
What will your mailing look like?
Make it good advertising – be proud of it
Prepare for the second stage

Think small, think close

The first thing to realise about direct mail is that the most effective results come from targeting the right – most appropriate – message to the right – most appropriate – people. We'll look more closely at this in Chapter 2, but for now, be aware that junk mail is the very last thing you want to create because it is the very last thing anybody will want to get.

> ❝ *I used to grab mailing lists from everywhere I could. It was a stupid, stupid mistake. Every time I mailed my own Customer lists I reaped huge rewards. Every time I went outside, I got much lower results. If I had just concentrated on meeting all the needs of my existing Customers, I would have saved myself a fortune.* ❞
> **– Mervyn West, Retailer**

Do you like junk mail? Of course you don't. Nobody does. So think about what you consider to be junk mail. It's not usually about the quality of what you have been sent – it is about the relevance it has to your life or your work, to you as an individual.

Junk isn't relevant and relevant isn't junk.

Broken down by age and sex

It's an old adage in direct mail that your lists should be broken down by age and sex! However, there is some truth behind it. Any list, whether it is your own Customer list or a list you have procured from elsewhere, is actually a group of individuals. Some of those individuals will have something in common. They might like to buy deluxe items. They might prefer to order by phone. They might hate you phoning them. They might be of a certain age. They might be men or women of a certain age.

Look to see whether you can break the lists you have down into smaller groups with something in common. This is called segmentation. The more segmentation you can do, the more opportunity you have to ensure that you are not in the junk mail business because you can use the smaller groups of similar people to change your message to suit what you know about them.

Let's take the example of a car dealer. They know what model their Customers have bought, they know how old the car is and they know when it was bought. From their service records they know the mileage and how frequently it is serviced. They know a great deal about the preferences of their Customers (manual or automatic, saloon or estate, price range, new or second-hand buyers), all of which they can use to make the message more relevant and appropriate to that Customer's buying habits.

Think close

There are only three kinds of Customer in the world: those you've got; those you used to have; and those you haven't got yet. In marketing speak, these are *Existing Customers*, *Lapsed Customers* and *prospects*. In terms of where you will find the highest response rates – and therefore the most likely chances of success – the order is as follows:

- ○ **Existing Customers – they offer your highest chance of success.**
- ○ **Lapsed Customers – the secret with this group is to convince them that you have solved whatever the problem or issue was that caused them to move on.**
- ○ **Prospects – cold (or non-Customer) lists will pull much lower response rates, often only achieving results of about one tenth of what you get from Customers.**

> Statistics prove that as long as you are able to convince them that you have solved the problem, lapsed Customers can become even more loyal than Customers who have never had a problem! Logic suggests that if this is true, you should upset Customers in order to have something to apologise for and put right. They'll love you for it.
>
> **Don't even think about it!!**

The position of prospects at the bottom of the response rate list doesn't mean that it is not worth mailing non-Customers. If you can make it work with prospects, you can get up to ten times more from Customers.

So keep it close and always put your existing Customers at the top of the list – literally!

Notice that I used the word *result* instead of *response* when I said you might get around a tenth the result from prospects than you do from Customers.

For clarity, I have differentiated them. *Response* tends to mean the number of enquiries or all orders coming in and by *result* I am referring to the finished position – when the salesforce have taken the orders and the invoices have been issued and paid. If you are trying to sell mail order or direct, it's the same. Response is the phone calls, faxes, order forms and e-mails you get – and result is what's left after people have changed their minds, sent it back and asked for refunds.

How much can you afford to spend?

Whatever the reason for your mailing, you should calculate – before you think about anything else – the amount of money you can afford to spend. You can do this quite simply. All you then have to do is make the response and result rates you have used for your calculation happen in reality. If this is your first attempt, don't worry! You will soon get a feel for what is achievable. But to start with, think modestly. You might think you have come up with the best offer in the world and at least half your Customers would kill to get it, but it is rarely the case.

Direct mail is a low response medium. The responders are nearly always the minority, response rates over 10 per cent are rare, over 20 per cent exceptional and over 30 per cent worth bragging about! There is no such thing as a good or bad response rate. It either works for you – with your sales processes and costs – or it doesn't. Only rely on your own experience or figures; never someone else's.

What you have to calculate is the allowable cost per result that you want – and then translate that into a budget. It is not difficult, and I strongly advise you to do this at the start. You will find, like most direct mailers, that it is easiest to work in costs and results per thousand (or, if you are a small mailer, per hundred).

You can calculate cost per response and cost per result. Cost per result is more useful, although it is slightly more complicated to calculate and you have to wait a little longer. Cost per response gives you a faster feedback and after a while you can develop an instinct about the conversion rates from response to result.

> Cost per response = The cost divided by the number of replies.

> Cost per result = The cost divided by the number of sales/orders/successful results.

The cost per result calculation should include all conversion costs: sales visits (salaries and other direct overheads); brochure costs; phone calls; and so on.

❝ It took me a little while to grasp the relationship between cost per response and cost per result. But once I had, I realised that what I said in the mailing and the kind of offers I made could change the gearing between the two. I could actually determine whether I wanted loads of enquiries of low to medium quality and leave the selling to the salesforce or, if we were short of salespeople, change it for a much more qualified but lower response rate. ❞
– Geoff Crane, Sales Manager, Office Equipment Co

If you don't do these sums before you begin, you only have yourself to blame for bad surprises.

If you are looking for results:

❑ Are you sure that you have done your sums up front?
❑ How much can you afford to spend per result?
❑ What is the average order value?
❑ How many orders do you need per thousand (or per hundred) mailed?
❑ What budget can you allow for this?

If you are generating leads or enquiries:

❑ How much can you afford to spend per result?
❑ How many results do you need per thousand?
❑ What is the conversion rate from enquiry to result?
❑ What is the cost per conversion?
❑ How many enquiries must you get?
❑ How much can you afford to spend getting each enquiry?
❑ What budget can you allow for this?

Remember, it is quite acceptable to place some value on the advertising effect for your business or for new Customer acquisition. Many successful mail order businesses are happy to make a new Customer sale at break-even or perhaps a small loss because they know from experience that the lifetime value of a Customer makes it worth while.

What do you want to do?

There are five principal reasons for using direct mail. Which of these is yours?

○ Lead generation: you want to obtain an enquiry about your product or service, which you then follow up with a visit, a phone call or a further mail-pack of information.
○ Mail order: you want to put forward a direct proposition or offer, which people can respond to by phone, writing, e-mail or fax.
○ Footfall or traffic: you are writing to invite people to a sale, exhibition or event, which you want them to visit.
○ To modify the relationship (usually with a longer term view to making a sale).
○ To inform or advertise: you want to tell people something new or different about yourself, your product or service.

What will your mailing look like?

This is about what direct mailers describe as format. Format is simply what size you will use, how many things you will put in the envelope and what they are there to do.

> How do you open your mail? Most people do it backwards. They look first at the address to see who it's for (and if you got their name right – you have much less chance from then on if you didn't!), and then they turn the envelope over to open it. The way that most people enclose their mail means when people open the envelope the first thing they see is the back or bottom of something. Turn it round! Come out with a smile and a handshake!

A format that works a treat for lead generation

Although I'm not comfortable with formula produced work, here's a format idea that works a treat. It achieves the huge benefit of giving the recipient a simple package to handle and understand, presents itself in a logical and sensible order, saves money, AND is easy to respond to! These are all such strong plus points that it has a lot going for it.

So you see what happens in the diagram opposite. Recipients see the message alongside the window, which has their name and address showing through. They turn over (perhaps another message?) and open. As they take the contents out, the letter folded the way it's shown in the diagram presents your big opening – the headline – and already grabs their attention. Use a Z-fold because, if they do flip it to have a quick look without unfolding it, the sales message is the right way up. And make sure there's a good strong PS working for you at the tail.

You'll also notice that, if we consider the roles of the pieces, the letter is the salesman and the leaflet tells you more and expands the information. The reply device is next, all but ready to return. Everything is in the right order. I usually recommend a straight forward business reply design and that side of the card should face back. Thus, it won't divert anybody who's having a quick flick through. It also simultaneously flags that it is the last piece and

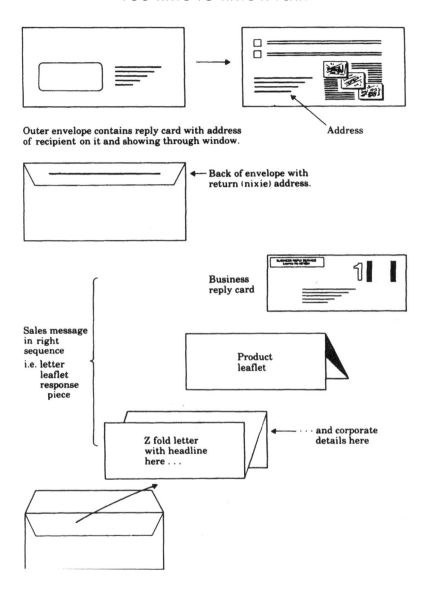

Outer envelope contains reply card with address
of recipient on it and showing through window.

Address

◄— Back of envelope with
return (nixie) address.

Business
reply card

Sales message
in right
sequence
i.e. letter
    leaflet
    response
    piece

Product
leaflet

◄— . . . and corporate
details here

Z fold letter
with headline
here . . .

that a reply is awaited. Now all the reader has to do is decide
whether they want to reply.

Assuming that they do, they'll find that you've already done the
donkey work and put their name and address on the reply card,
making it quick and easy for them to tick a box or two and pop it

in the post back to you. Since the card is this way round it's ideally suited for the window envelope I mentioned earlier.

Choosing a format is important – there is much more on this at the end of Chapter 5.

Make it good advertising – be proud of it

One of the fastest ways to relegate your direct mail to junk mail is to ignore the powerful advertising effect it can have. And it is free! That is to say, if you are going to use direct mail to get enquiries, orders or invite people to something, make sure you play to the whole audience. Recognise from the outset that there will be three categories of reader on your list: 'yes', 'no' and 'maybe' readers.

> **Aim your mailing at 'maybe' readers! 'Yes' readers love you and will respond anyway. 'No' readers hate you and whatever you send will be junk to them. 'Maybe' readers are your next Customers and your growth potential.**

Understand that when people hold your mailing, they hold your business. Your mailing is delivering the only evidence that you are as good as you say you are. Everything contributes to that feeling within the reader's mind and heart: weight of paper, colour, feel, typestyles, photos, and so on.

> **Create a mailing you can feel proud of. If you know you have shown off your business and your offer as best as you possibly can within the budget available, you can't do more. If you're not sure, why not ask a few Customers and see what they think!**

ALWAYS include a letter. At least, never leave a letter out unless you have a very good reason. Letters get higher readership than anything else.

The function of the letter is to lead and explain offers and propositions. The brochure then gives supporting information and further details and the reply card brings in the orders or enquiries.

If you then want to add more items or even three dimensional gimmicks and attention grabbers, that's fine. But make sure they have a clear function link to the core message.

❝ We used to offer all manner of incentives and gimmicks to entice people to our seminars and workshops. Then we tested a certificate of training. It was incredibly effective. And just because it linked so directly to our product ❞
– Julia Fraser, Conference Organiser, TGR Organisation

Prepare for the second stage

It is always wise to plan the follow up and response handling before you release your mailing. If you have salespeople let them see the mailing, tell them when it is to be released and familiarise them with what they are supposed to do with the replies. Do the same for the switchboard or telesales team. If you are offering information make sure it is printed and ready. If it's a product you're promoting, have stocks ready.

Here's a good idea to get fulfilment packages taken more seriously. It works extremely well – and will hardly cost you anything. Depending on the quantities you're dealing with it can be achieved for no more than the cost of having a rubber stamp made, or some labels printed, or even just a small piece of artwork to add to your existing envelope message.

What you're going to achieve is an instant lift in the reader's eyes. You can obviously put a little creative thought into how you do it, but these are the basic magic words that will achieve this extra effect on those who have requested details from you:

"Here is the information you requested"

When fulfilling requests for information or fulfilling the second stage of a two-stage sell, most of what is said elsewhere – tactically, strategically and creatively – applies. These are, after all, only a mailing of a different sort. And the first, often overlooked, difference is that they come after you have spent good advertising money stimulating the interest and because they go to red hot prospects. This is your big chance to make a sale or to set one up for the future. That is why I believe that you should take as much time, trouble and effort over the fulfilment as you did over the original advertising, if not more.

Making the most of your fulfilment pack

Think about what the reader wants – yes, they want more information, but what else? Inspiration? Reassurance? Advice? Help? You must give them all of these things. But you must not stop there. You must offer them more: by phone, by mail, by visit, or at a nearby outlet. You must be felt to be caring, interested, understanding and, above all, approachable.

Think about what you want too. But do so from the recipients' point of view.

Don't overcook it. Too much communication is as bad as too little. And always do everything you can to be appropriate.

It's no good just plonking a confusing mass of information in front of them. Think about how to present it in a clear, logical and convincing way. Use your accompanying letter to lead people, not just through the sales story but, quite literally, through the materials you are sending.

Also, think about what you want in terms of their response. And sell that idea to them. Make a proposition. Describe the action you want from them and justify it. Give them reasons to do it.

Achieve these four ideals:

○ **Make the action attractive**
○ **Make the action sensible**
○ **Make the action clear**
○ **Make the action simple**

And whatever else you do, don't forget to start by thanking them for contacting you!

1. **Start your direct mail experiences with your existing Customers – they will be your highest response group. Second come lapsed Customers, and last are new prospects.**

2. You can use segmentation to break lists down into smaller, homogeneous groups, which you can target more closely by varying the message as appropriate. Segmentation enables you to be interesting to more people.

3. Junk mail is mail that isn't relevant. Relevant mail isn't junk.

4. Mailings are measured by cost per response and cost per result. Cost per result is the ultimate measure.

5. Simple mathematics enables you to check whether you can make a profit and also what results justify what budgets. A little experience can be gained easily by releasing a few advances of the mailing up front to see what happens.

6. In deciding what format to use, bear in mind the information you have to impart and the size of any existing materials you want to include. Letters almost always earn their weight in gold!

7. Remember, when people hold your mailing, they hold you, and your business. The difference between a mailing that is good advertising and one that is not is insignificant in cost but huge in effect. The advertising effect comes free and works on many, many more than just those who respond. To create good advertising, create something you and the business can be proud of.

8. Always prepare your fulfilment and response handling before the mailing goes out. Have stocks ready and tell everyone involved what you are doing, and when.

9. If you are sending a fulfilment pack – further information – in response to the mailing, follow the advice this book offers for preparing a mailing. Remember, it is even more important, since the fulfilment is what transforms your earlier investment into profit. Don't forget to say thank you for their reply!

What's in this chapter for you

How important is targeting?
Segmentation, personalisation and customisation
Lists to avoid
Where to find lists – and what to ask about them
The list buyer's checklist

How important is targeting?

Research has clearly identified the database – and therefore using data for targeting – as the single wisest thing you can spend direct mail money on. The list of priorities goes like this:

Targeting	500%
Proposition	200%
Timing	100%
Creative design	35%
Response device	25%

Let me explain the percentages. A well-known international direct marketing agency carried out some research to find out not only which were the most important response building factors, but also by how much they differed. The results were quite surprising.

The agency examined the difference between a mailing with a good response device (reply card, order form, and so on) and a mailing with a poor one. They compared the results of mailings with good creative design and bad creative design, and so on. The percentage is the increased response gained from a mailing that was a good example. Thus it can be seen that a mailing with a good response device could pull as much as 25 per cent more response than a similar mailing with a poor one.

It is remarkable therefore that the whole creative design area should come second to bottom from the list. Most people imagine that creative design has far more leverage than a mere 35 per cent (actually, there is a catch to it which I'll come back to).

The reason I am showing you this research is to emphasise where your priorities should lie. Look at the figures again. They show you quite clearly the importance of timing (see Chapter 3), the importance of constructing a proposition (also Chapter 3), and, most significantly, the vital importance of targeting. When you are prioritising your financial investment in direct mail, be guided by these figures. The one area that is definitely worth your investment, whether it is in time or money, is that at the very top of the list! It is way ahead of anything else. Don't skimp on lists or your database.

The creative design paradox

The factors researched were only those that built response. They paid no attention whatsoever to whether the mailing was a good piece of advertising and effectively conveyed brand and image values. This is the advertising effect of your mailing, which, as I have already explained, goes to work even on those who are not responding directly to the mailing. This is very powerful and its value places creativity much higher on the list of priorities than this research shows. But be clear, targeting remains well out in front!

> ❝ People ask me what is the difference between a list and a database. I remember reading that a list is the whereabouts of an audience. Their names and addresses. A database is the whereabouts and the whatabouts of people. In other words all the other information we can glean which might be useful for targeting ❞
> **– Sally Peterson, Small Business Advisor**

Hunting out software

It is simply common sense that you need a computer to store and maintain your Customer and prospect details. Indeed, most office software programs come with a basic database facility built in.

In Microsoft Word, for example, there is a simple database and mail merge capability. However, also available are Customer and prospect database systems, which enable you to track sales leads and store Customer information. Depending on the number of your records, you should consider these systems. They are not expensive and can be invaluable to your direct mail activity.

❝ I went to one of JFR's courses and really took on board what he said about targeting and personalisation. I was surprised to find that, even with my small database of just a few hundred, I could use my regular software to target and to personalise – and even customise to some extent – the mailings which I sent out. It really, really worked. ❞
– Elaine Wood, CMB Image Consultant

Why is Customer and prospect information so important?

A major role for direct mail lies in the nurturing of Customer relationships. Customers are no longer content to be faceless units of sale. Quite rightly, they are placing significant demand on the businesses they patronise to be treated as individuals and to be recognised for the value they are.

So the days of 'Dear Sir or Madam' or even 'Dear Customer' are gone. Customers now expect a more personal and, to some degree, more intimate communication; intimate in the sense that it speaks to them and them only. Thus, database information is used to add both relevance and recognition.

❝ I knew it wasn't junk mail. I have received and bought from their catalogue for years. And anyway their letter mentioned the actual items I bought last year. ❞
– Eunice Gibson, Granny (and Catalogue Buyer)

What Customer information could be significant for you: what dates, financial information, personal information or preferences? Make a list. Check out what you have and what you don't have. Then devise a programme to fill in the holes. Ask questions of your Customers when they visit. Gather information by phone or write and ask them. Don't be intrusive. Let the information emerge at a natural, comfortable rate.

Segmentation, personalisation and customisation

The idea of segmentation is that you use information stored on your database to identify smaller discrete groups of Customers with significant common attributes. Only you will know what is significant for your Customers and your business.

If we return to the example of the motor dealer (Chapter 1), such attributes might be: price range; model; manual/automatic; always a new car/always used/varies; saloon/estate, and so on.

Segmentation is used to target Customers in two ways: to include them in or out of the mailing; and to change the message and/or proposition to those we have selected. By using segmentation, mailings will be more relevant, offer a more attractive proposition and reflect the nature of the Customer relationship.

Let's consider an example.

> **Dear Mr Squires,**
>
> **GREAT NEWS!**
>
> **When you test drive the new Primo you qualify for a valuable 'third purchase' bonus guaranteeing you a discount of £500.00.**
>
> **It's now almost two years since you bought your last Primo. And thanks to your policy of regular servicing and maintenance, you have preserved its value at a premium for a vehicle with under 50,000 miles on the clock.**
>
> **For you, the release of the new Super Primo couldn't be more timely or better value. Not only is this the perfect moment to trade in, but waiting for you is a guaranteed personal 'thank you for your custom' bonus worth at least £500.00.**

You can imagine how the letter continues specifically playing back the data we have from the Customer record, using it to add relevance and recognition. At this level, we have gone beyond personalisation (the simple addition of name, address and personal salutation) into customisation. You can claim to have reached the customisation stage when you can look at the text and see that only one or two Customers are getting the same or even similar letters.

Nothing in this example letter cannot be achieved by even the most basic mail merge software.

Data protection

In most countries, if you are storing Customer or prospect information on computer, you must register with a data protection authority and comply with data protection laws. Often, if you maintain records manually, there is no need to register.

Do you have a list or database?

You can often use information from other sources to transform your list into a database. For example, if the list of Customers in the sales office were to be populated with information gleaned from invoices in the accounts department, you would have a sensational database capability!

So far we've considered a lot about Customer and prospect information that, in one way or another, your business might already have. They are from internal sources. Now it is time to look outside the business at external sources so that you can add new names to your database.

Affinity lists

Partnerships with other businesses that are interested in similar types of people can be extremely profitable for both parties. You swap information with the partner and then write to Customers explaining why.

For example, a local sports shop might swap its list of Customers with a local health club. The health club mails the retailer's Customers, offering, say, a discount on the joining fee because they are Customers of the sports shop. In return, the sports shop mails the club members with a voucher in recognition of the fact that they are members of the health club.

The list swap example highlights the issue of duplication. Some health club members may already use the sports shop. And vice versa. The two list owners need to decide what to do with these mutual Customers. The most foolish thing would be to leave them out. Because they are on both lists they are ideal repeat business potential for both. Is there something we could do for their family or circle of friends?

> The more duplication there is between your list and any other, the better potential that list represents. The presence of duplicates in greater numbers means that the profile of those on that list is closer to yours.
>
> Look for duplication – it's good news about a list you are considering. But, of course, you should treat them differently. Nobody wants to get two letters from you. Especially when they are the same!!

Lists to avoid

There seems to be a certain fascination with mailing generalised lists. The presidents and managing directors of the *Fortune* 500 in the USA and the *Times* Top 1000 in the UK, for example, must rate amongst the most mailed people in the world. Most often such lists, although widely available and sometimes even free, will simply waste your mailing budget because they are just not specific enough.

The same often applies to associations and chambers of commerce. Rubbish bins around the world are littered with mailings from local businesses 'writing to introduce' themselves to other local businesses, saying, pretty much, 'buy from us because we're local too'. YAWN!

> Targeting is about finding reasons why prospects are suited to buying from your business – beyond the mere fact that you exist!

Where to find lists – and what to ask about them

Apart from those found from affinities or partnerships, lists are generally available from four sources:

- ○ List owners, who market their own lists.
- ○ List managers, who are paid by list owners to look after and market their lists.
- ○ List brokers, who live off commission on their sales of lists.
- ○ List compilers (for example directory publishers and specialist – like medical or education – list companies).

Brokers and compilers will nearly always provide you with the information on disk or labels. Owners and managers may insist that you give them the materials to mail.

Be clear that owners and managers will always have their own interests first and foremost. Brokers and compilers survive through you being satisfied and coming back for more.

Become a name magpie!

Make sure that your business becomes a name and address magpie. Every time someone contacts your business, even if they don't buy, gather basic contact information. A list of people who contacted you because they were thinking of enquiring or buying from you will always contain better prospects than an outsourced list of people who may never have heard of you.

The list buyer's checklist

There are a number of questions you should ask before you rent a list. Specifically you will need to know about costs, timing and availability, how the list is supplied, to whom they are prepared to release it, what other mailings (especially from competitors) have preceded you and what limitations apply. I suggest that before you place any order, verbal or written, you examine the rental contract in detail.

Lists start to deteriorate the moment you buy them. The list owner may have ways of updating the list, you probably won't. Around 35 per cent of ladies' hairdressers and florists go out of business each year. The average company director or VP stays in the job just two and a half years, so they are turning over at 40 per cent per annum as well!

Remember that the purchase price of a list can be five or six times the rental cost. And remember, too, that you only rent enough to do the test – you only go back for more if it works.

> ❝ *It was my first attempt, and I just didn't realise. So I rented the whole list. Then a friend suggested we just mail a few to start with. We got one reply. One!! It was just more money down the drain to mail the rest. If only I'd just tested the minimum quantity to start with. Nowadays, with new lists, I try some, then I try some more, then – if it's working well – I go for the full thing.* ❞
> **– Geoff Crane, Sales Manager, Office Equipment Co**

What you need to know

The first question you need to ask is: 'Where did the names come from?' Even in these sophisticated days you can still see the odd red face when you ask this simple and basic question. Remember that, for every penny you spend with the broker, you may spend ten to twenty more on the production and mailing costs – so their answers matter.

When was the list compiled or created, is it an ongoing process, and how is the file updated? Lists are living entities; they need new names added to keep them fresh and a constant or very regular updating process to keep them clean. Does the list owner, for example, use and encourage others to use, an 'if undelivered please return to' request on the envelope? When they mail, do they ask for and facilitate replies that seek new address and other data changes?

How often is the list mailed? What responses are obtained? Remember here that lists usually become more responsive with use, not less. But ask what sort of responses others have obtained, in what situation, and with what products or services. Don't necessarily be satisfied with the answers you get and, if you're in any doubt or suspicious, ring the advertisers and ask them.

Ask whether it is a list of purchasers (or subscribers) or responders or enquirers. Purchasers or subscribers who have paid will usually be better than those who haven't or those who have simply enquired and not converted to sale. All can work, but generally the buyers are best. Cash buyers are usually better than credit users.

What quantities or assessments of deliverability are given, and is there any rebate or refund for nixies (undelivered and gone-aways)? Although few list owners will guarantee a percentage of deliverability, they should be prepared to give you some assessment. The most conscientious will offer to refund all or part of the postage to get the gone-aways back. Some will only offer this if nixies exceed the assessed level – and often they will only refund the excess.

After your test, how many more are there left to mail and are there any discounts for multiple or volume use? The more the better, since the volume lowers roll-out production costs and possibly lowers product or service provision costs too.

Also check whether they can 'flag' the names you have tested, either for further analysis after the mailing, or so that, if you choose, you can leave them out of the roll out.

In what form can the list be supplied? Is it available for merge/purge?

Lastly, you need to know what their minimum test quantities are and what the costs will be for two activities: the test and a roll-out, if successful. Remember to evaluate your test against roll-out cost projections and not test costs.

1. **Research shows that targeting is the most cost effective place to invest your direct mail money.**
2. **Creative copy and design are still more effective than the figures suggest since the advertising effect works on non-responders as well as responders.**
3. **Database information enables direct mail to play a major role in nurturing Customer relationships. It should add relevance and recognition.**
4. **Segmentation enables the identification of small discrete Customer groups. Customisation is the variation of individual communications enabled by what we know about them.**

5. Lists can be built from internal information or acquired externally. The most valuable are usually internal. Partnerships with other businesses with similar Customer profiles create affinity opportunities.

7. A 'magpie attitude' to contact information is valuable.

8. Ask questions that ensure the list you are acquiring will be appropriate and good value.

What's in this chapter for you

Making the most of timing
A proposition or an offer?
The basics of testing
The 'What to test' checklist
Coding your replies

Making the most of timing

Consumer mail is best received (not mailed) on Friday or Saturday; next best is Thursday. My advice is aim for Friday.

Business-to-business mail is best received on a Wednesday: Tuesday and Thursday are next best; Monday and Friday are worst; Saturday for most businesses becomes Monday!

You should have an understanding of postal timings and just how accurate these are. The UK and USA are comparatively well served. In most places 'you gets what you pay for' prevails – so the more precise you want the timing, the greater the cost.

Mail for all seasons

In direct marketing we experience two response 'windows'. These are two periods when responses will be markedly better than the rest. They are (give or take the odd week!) the second week of January until the first week of June. And the second week of September until the second week of November. Of course, they are not dead cut-offs. Overlay this experience against your own and any seasonal aspect of the products.

If you are in mail order, short daylight periods or rain will help, as indeed will any kind of inclement weather. But just take it as a bonus! Holiday weekends are something of a problem. Some report excellent results: others, catastrophes.

A proposition or an offer?

Understand the power of a proposition. Nearly all direct mail includes a proposition. After all, if you want to rouse someone to take the action you want, there is nothing like an attractive or acceptable proposition to do it.

If you want a response, then you must give me something to respond about; something to say 'yes' to. Make me an offer. If it's a good one, I'll accept. To be clear, I tend to use the word 'proposition' to mean what it says and 'offer' when it's a special offer or enhanced proposition. Take my advice – include a proposition, preferably an offer.

> *Every advertising message should make an offer. It's the offer that suggests the action. And if the offer is put across thoughtfully, it will more than suggest action – it will close the sale.*
> **– Scott Hamble, Insurance Broker**

Offer has, of course, two meanings. We know about offer in the sense of a proposition (take my advice –include one!). But there is also an offer in the sense of a 'special offer' available to you, and very potent that is too. We all like to receive something a little extra; something for nothing; something to reward us for placing our business with you.

> *I had a mailing today from my hearing aid people. It said, 'Your birthday is in the next few days so please accept these free batteries as a gift from us'. Brilliant!*
> **– Hard of hearing friend**

Just about all else that matters

1 Think a great deal about constructing a proposition that people will want to accept. The more you can do to relate that proposition to your audience (or segments of audience) the better it will work.
2 Consider what you can do to enhance the proposition with an offer that will attract action and have a clearly established link with the product/service that you are selling, or the people you are selling to. Why not both?
3 Develop a clear and explicit rationale for both proposition and offer.
4 Sell it. Sell the proposition rather than the product or service. Sell it in front. Sell it first. Sell it fast. And sell it thoroughly.

The basics of testing

Testing falls into formal or informal testing. The sad thing about formal testing is that most books – including others I have written – cover it in detail showing you how to calculate test cell sizes, select confidence levels and do all manner of other wonderful things. It often comes across as quite complicated and the calculations put people off. Formal testing is used by those mailing large quantities regularly. In this book I will concentrate on informal testing.

If you would like details of formal testing, e-mail me at jfr@jfr.co.uk. All you need to type is 'TESTING 60+' and I'll know what you want.

Informal testing

By informal I mean two things: first, it is often the only kind of testing smaller direct mail users can do; and second, it might not stand up to statistical scrutiny.

Test only one or two things at a time: one letter versus another; one offer versus another. To test, divide your total mailing into two or three segments (usually referred to as 'cells'). Big mailers are able to consider quantities of 5,000 or even 10,000 per cell. Medium and smaller mailers cannot. Keep it simple. Read on for advice about 'control cells' and 'bankers' and whether to believe the results or not.

In the graveyard of classic tests

❑ A new product feature or design that the manufacturer or supplier *knows* is better than the old one. But the consumer likes the old one; they are familiar with it. In fact, they are reluctant and resistant to change.
❑ A new gift or premium which seems to offer the prospective buyer temptation beyond delight, whereas what they actually see is too good a deal, which makes them suspicious of the offer and destroys credibility.
❑ A price-cut or discount which equally destroys credibility, or worse, shatters the perception of value for money, or re-positions the product so drastically (from say, luxury to bargain) that they no longer want it.

There is a constant need to search out and discover, to push progress and innovation. But each time you fall on a prospective 'improvement' , no matter how spectacular it seems, view it with intense suspicion – until it's tested!

The four most important things to remember when testing

- Concentrate on testing the major items: these always centre around the list, the offer, the product, the timing, and the (creative) package. The most overrated of these is creative: the most underrated is timing.
- Test big differences to get big differences. Two similar creative approaches will yield two similar results; two similar lists will yield two similar results; and so on.
- Don't do what others do. Test results are invariably very individual. Your results tell you, at any given time, what your Customers or prospects respond to from you and only you. There are inevitably some general tactics and ideas that work well for the majority. But it only takes 51 per cent to be a majority!
- Don't look for too much logic behind test results. There's an awful lot of emotion in a purchase decision. The head may be logical and therefore more predictable, but the heart is a different matter.

The concept of 'the banker'

Testing is an inherently risky business. The overriding priority must be to protect the maximum amount of your investment from the unknown, untried and unproven.

The overall policy should be to change from the known as little as possible.

The discovery of something that works better is exciting and tempting. Imagine that you've been doing things in a particular way for some time when along comes a better product, a new technique, a creative approach, a list, that seems to offer a significantly better result. "Why," asks the manager, "should you do it the old way when we can now offer this new one? It has to be better."

The answer is that although new ideas may seem to offer improvement, you never know until you've tried them. Time after time in my career, I have watched things that everyone thought would prove not just better, but substantially better, go out on test and end up in the graveyard.

Make sure you have a control cell in your test

For your test to have any real significance or relevance to the status quo, you must include the status quo in your test. The reason you need to do this is to obliterate doubt – or at least quantify it! You must therefore place the status quo, in effect a control, in the same environment.

It must be mailed at the same time, in the same conditions as your tests. Then you will be able to determine where you are, where you came from, and – if you have your test priorities right – where you're going. And therefore, hopefully, what you should be testing next.

> ❝ *I ignored advice about testing with a control. Then I realised I didn't know where I had gone from – or where I was going to! Don't make the same mistake!* ❞
> **Jerry Gordon, Marketing Manager, Magazine Publisher**

The 'what to test' checklist

As well as *lists* and *timing*, think about testing:

- ○ Strategy
- ○ Mail order v salesforce (or retailers)
- ○ One stage v two stage sale
  Note: a lot of products need to be sold in two stages, the first stage being the generation of enquiry, and the second, following a response to stage one, the conversion to sale. Although this introduces further expense into the proceedings, this can be more than offset by:
  - a substantial cost saving in many cases, since complex or expensive sales materials are directed at those who have expressed a clear interest in what you have to sell and are, therefore, more likely to buy
  - building you a list of prospects for repeat approach on this product or fresh approaches on other products. It often provides you with useful additional information to make the future approaches on a more timely, relevant and appropriate basis.
- ○ Product
- ○ Deluxe v regular

Do you offer the deluxe as the main proposition with an economy option? Or the regular as the main proposition with a deluxe option? That's the test! It's worth noting that a deluxe version will generally be taken up by about 30 to 40 per cent of people.

○ Offer
○ No gift incentive v discount v none
○ High price v low(er!)
○ Cash v credit v credit cards
   Note: when testing cash v credit v credit cards, if you can't test all three, test both types of credit sale first. Then whichever wins should be tested against the two cash versions: cash enclosed and bill me later).
○ Creative design
○ Hard sell v soft
○ Four colour process v two or three colour
○ Photography v illustration
○ Personalisation – with v without
○ Copy length – short v long
○ Headlines
   Note: although the current trend is to credit creative design with a lot less influence than was previously thought, I have seen response improvements of 500 and 600 per cent from simple headline tests.
○ Format
○ Reply paid v not
   Note: this one has more to do with the balance of quantity and quality than the cost. Personally, I think you should pay. It's called courtesy!
○ Address placing
   Note: On the outer envelope? On the letter to look personal-ised? On the response device to make it easier to return? This can make a world of difference to response. If you only have one option or can only afford one option, make it the reply device and use a window envelope.

Don't believe everything your testing tells you! If you get a differential between results of less than 15 per cent (for example 2 per cent and 2.3 per cent), don't believe it. Test again.

Code the variants

If you don't code the test variants to distinguish one from the other, you could have problems. In fact there are two reasons to code: the first is to ensure that your mailing test variations go out correctly; the second is to enable you to tell which variations are doing what.

Contents codes

Many people test items that will change several pieces of print. Thus contents codes are printed on all items to ensure the right letter goes with the right leaflet goes with the right reply card – and they all get enclosed into the right envelope. A typical contents coding system might look like this:

$$14/8\text{-}01/A/4/3$$

Here's how it is made up:

14/	Promotion code		
8-01/	Month and year of mailing		
A/	Offer A, B, C, and so on		
4/	List 1, 2, 3, 4, and so on		
3	Component number:	1	outer envelope
		2	letter
		3	reply slip
		4	gift voucher
		5	reply envelope

Response codes

Whether you decide to have full contents codes or not, the item you really can't escape coding is the reply piece. If you're looking for a telephone response you'll have to find some ingenious way of measuring the difference. I guess the most common of all is the Jill Blake/Laura Good method. Phone and ask for Jill Blake – you're a code A! Ask for Laura Good – you're a code B! Or have dedicated telephone numbers for each code.

Use scratch coding; it's cheaper than changes to printing plates. Make sure the code only alters in one colour. Make sure that every single piece of the package carries the code. This cuts down the risk of incorrect pieces being included in incorrect packages. Below is an example of a cheap coding system for litho printing. To get ten different codes the printer merely has to stop the machine at the required quantities and delete one numeral from the plate.

0123456789	Code 9
012345678	Code 8
01234567	Code 7
0123456	Code 6
012345	Code 5

1. Mail to consumers is best sent to arrive around the weekend – for business, aim for midweek.
2. There are higher response seasons: January to June is the highest, followed by September to November.
3. Every mailing should make a proposition. Propositions work hardest when enhanced with special offers or discounts.
4. Testing is a significant benefit of direct mail. Small and medium direct mail users can use 'informal testing' methods.
5. Testing priorities are: lists (or segmentation); timing; offers; and creative approaches. To get big results, test big differences.
6. Be sure to code the variations of your tests on the reply piece – if it's a complex test or mix of different enclosures code all the matching pieces to get the right things in the right envelopes.
7. Scratch coding saves money – and don't let your printer charge you for it. He owes you a favour – you gave him the order!

What's in this chapter for you

How your readers read
Building a copy structure
Do's and don'ts for good copy
Guidelines for design and layout
Designer do's and don'ts
Answering reader's questions
Getting letter perfect
Checklist for replies

How your readers read

Most written advertising – direct response or other – is tackled by its reader in three distinct phases. They are the *glance*, the *scan*, the *read*.

The most important point about this theory is that readers have a 'gearbox' in their head that has only three positions: yes, maybe and no.

The next most important point is that you must put your proposition up front. If you're going to ask people to give you their time, they should at least know what's in it for them. The job of copy and design is to present your proposition and to persuade as many readers as possible to accept it.

You need to recognise that we must achieve success not once, not twice, but three times as our readers go through the three stages of reading. We must succeed as they glance at it – to get them to move on. We must succeed when they scan it – to get them to move on. And we must succeed when they read it – to get them to absorb, accept and act.

The number of readers will decrease at each stage. But you have to make sure that, as the numbers dwindle, your effort increases its influence on those who remain.

Glance, scan, read

The early glancing process is a horrendously fast event. The eye rests on a number of points for just two tenths of a second. The tolerance level per A4 spread is about 10 eye-resting points. Your mailing lives or dies in just two seconds! With an A3 spread the tolerance level goes up to about 15. So you have three seconds. Then, with the speed of light, the glancers brain makes a decision —go again or quit?

The second trip round, the scan, gives you more time. The scan is all about gathering evidence to justify a read. It will include more copy. The glance was picking up odd words and maybe a full phrase but not much else other than feeding the visual sense. Here whole headlines, photo-captions, and sub-heads will be read.

How you fare from here is up to you. With some you'll get the in-depth read. Some will still not decide without a preliminary fast read. Then they'll go for the body copy and diagrams and more complicated pictures and illustrations.

Building a copy structure

There are a couple of good structures for copy. As I said earlier, I am not a great believer in writing to a formula. I prefer to check what has been written to see if it meets the formula's concept.

However, the first structure worth bearing in mind is:

○ **AIDA: Attention, Interest, Desire, Action**

Or, more explicitly, grab attention first. Once you've got it, build interest levels. This keeps them with you. Then stimulate the desire for them to do what you are proposing. Finally, encourage action now.

The second formula for copy structure is my own favourite and the one which always unlocked a block for me. Courtesy of US direct marketing expert Bob Stone, his seven key points:

○ **Bob Stone's seven key points**
1. **Put the main benefit first.**
2. **Enlarge upon the main benefit, and bring in the secondary benefits.**

3. Tell the reader precisely what they will get.
4. Back up your story with case histories and endorsements.
5. Tell your reader what they might lose if they don't act.
6. Sum-up by re-stating the benefits – but in a different way.
7. Incite immediate action.

Distinguish between benefits and features. Benefits are what Customers actually buy – what your product or service will do for them – and therefore what you should sell. Features are what or how the benefits are achieved. To get the most enquiries stop at the benefits. If I need to know how something makes the benefit happen, then I have yet another reason to enquire. You also leave something for the salesperson to say that hasn't already been said. If you are going for a mail order sale, include all the benefits and all the features too.

What is positioning?

There was a two word headline in the papers recently. Potentially it was a contradiction. Yet because the advertiser has very well positioned themselves, they could get away with it.

The two word headline was simply … Harrods Sale.

Did I read the ads, check the prices and reductions, make any decisions expecting anything other than I found? Was I looking for prices cheaper than the chain stores or bargain basements? No. I was looking, not to pick up a bargain from Harrods, but for a Harrods bargain: a perfect piece of positioning.

❝ How do you achieve correct positioning? You must live and breathe it. In direct mail you achieve positioning by careful attention to everything. The typefaces. The tone of the voice. The nature of the offer. The weight, colour, feel of the paper. The quality of the design and print. Everything. ❞
– Tim Spencer, Direct Marketing Copywriter

The largest single difference between ordinary advertising copy and direct response advertising copy is that ours sells. What it sells is the proposition, reagardless of whether that proposition is that the reader should buy, enquire, or visit a store or exhibition.

In direct mail, copy is far, far more important than artwork. Pictures don't sell. Design doesn't sell. Pictures might explain, demonstrate, or illustrate. Those things help a sale: they don't make one. Pictures will certainly grab attention, and it's the use you make of their attention with your copy that is more important.

Design doesn't sell, not in direct mail. It positions. It supports copy. It displays your wares. It humanises, creates mood and eases the task of reading, but it doesn't sell. It certainly contributes; you might say it smoothes the way to the sale. But it doesn't sell.

The best copywriting advice I have ever given anybody was:

*Write what the reader wants to read and **not** what the writer wants to write*

Take this tip seriously and use it to question every decision. Seeing things from the reader's point of view, putting them first, will never do you any harm. It will always serve you in the end. So extend this simple philosophy way beyond the copy: to the graphics; to the development of the proposition; to the format – throughout!

Copy sells for you

Direct mail is a words medium. You will be amazed at the word-power that is available to you and at just how many words you can get people to read.

Very few good mailings feature anything near good writing. We chuck away the grammar text books. We ignore convention. We use punctuation in ways that would make English teachers cringe – not just for the sake of it, but just to be easy to read.

❝ *I suddenly realised it wasn't any different to any other kind of sales situation. I just had to do the same thing I usually do – but ON PAPER!* ❞
– Greg Clarke, one man mail order business.

Since I cannot write your copy for you, I'm now going to give you a comprehensive checklist of advice I have been given, thoughts I have developed, and experiences I have gained.

Do's and don'ts for good copy

Here are 17 do's and 10 don'ts. That's 27 ways to make your copy irresistible.

Do …

Prepare
- ○ Plan what you want to say – develop a rationale that would convince you to accept the offer, then work on it. But be flexible. Often you will stumble on a better, stronger or more appealing idea half way through what you have already started. Write both. And then choose.
- ○ Write long and edit back if you need to – *never* the other way round. If your copy runs short but you feel you did the job, the designer will be delighted! And the reader won't mind either. The PS is often the most read part of any letter – use it powerfully.

Write
- ○ Develop a flowing style – not smooth or bland, but pleasant and charming. In letters be conversational and personal without being impertinent or familiar.
- ○ Make yourself easy to read and understand – the easiest sentences to understand are just eight words long. At 32 words you've lost them.
- ○ Concentrate on communicating well – forget about grammar. Worry more about flow, being understood and communicating well. One acid test is to read copy aloud, or better still, get someone else to. Where this reader trips up so will others.
- ○ Be warm and sunny-natured – then let yourself shine through. It's infectious. Just as telesales people are advised to smile on the phone!

○ Avoid the crescendo – in 99 per cent of cases 'crescendo letters' should be stood on their head. Crescendo letters are those that gradually build up to their offer, finally blurting it out in the last paragraph. Readers do not start out interested. They start out indifferent. We have to earn their attention. They start out looking for excuses to bin us. The strongest way to come out fighting is to hit them with the biggest benefit first.

○ Use link-words and phrases – start paragraphs with them: and; but; also; what's more; for example. You may have had problems with this style at school, but school's out! And use punctuation and text marks too. There are all manner of devices ...

    ... which just tell the reader to keep going!

○ Use simple language – and simple construction. This kind of thing. It's so easy to handle. Especially in comparison with the much longer and, from a constructional aspect, markedly more complex style of sentences that barely give the unfortunate individual trying to cope with them a chance to breathe and which become, therefore, asphyxiating in more ways than one!

○ Use active words: tick; send; act; claim; take; grab; select.

○ Be ruthless – strip out waffle or padding. But be careful not to de-humanise, cool or get in the way of the flowing style. This is the yardstick: is it of benefit, is it interesting, does it convince, does it hold them, is it there to lubricate? If it doesn't do one of these, it doesn't deserve to get printed. You can often strike out whole paragraphs measuring against this yardstick.

Humanise

○ Humanise wherever possible – bring in personalities and names. Do away with 'our Sales Department can ...' Instead use 'Jenny Pearce, your personal Customer Service Manager can ...'

○ Snuggle up with the reader! Do away with '... it's got many features ...' . Instead use '... let's run through the features together ...'

○ Sprinkle the evergreen 'turn-on's' around plentifully: you; new; now; free; introducing; announcing; save. Use unique very carefully. It is an evergreen with severe leaf mould!

○ Picture your reader. Hold imaginary sales chats with them. Fantasise the sale in your head. And then write about it.

○ Paint word pictures – try to find words that are evocative and inspiring. Which would you buy, a policy that pays 'a regular monthly benefit' – or 'a fountain of money, placing hard cash in your hands each and every month?'

❍ Ensure the copy works on all three levels – glance, scan, read. Do this with the layout artist/designer. If you're not sure whether it succeeds use the 'snatch test'. Give it to someone. Count five seconds. Snatch it back. If they can't tell you what it's about, you've failed!

Don't ...

❍ Don't use incredible, or uncaring words or phrases. Avoid the time-weary as opposed to the time-honoured.
❍ Don't use word-play, puns or be clever. It doesn't work.
❍ Don't use too many 'me-words': I; my; we; our. It's supposed to be all about them, the reader! So by all means use enough of these to be personal, but don't go overboard. 'You' and 'your' are fine! They can be used as much as you like: especially at the beginning of paragraphs, a place where 'me' should only rarely be found.
❍ Don't use negative words. Change the aspect from which you are writing round to the positive.
❍ Don't use abstract or needlessly complex words and descriptions – do you really mean 'seating arrangements' – or chairs?
❍ Don't use etc. In a mailing it means you've left something unsaid or partially explained ... or worse, you've left the reader something to work out for themselves.
❍ Don't forget. You'll lose more readers in the first 50 words than you will in the rest. So turn up the heat. Put plenty of thought and effort into headlines. 'When you've written the headline you've spent 70% of the Client's budget'. This does not indicate the price of copywriting! It's to demonstrate how important the headline is.
❍ Don't worry about length of copy. Worry more about whether it's interesting, paced and easy to read.
❍ Don't leave questions unanswered. To the direct mail copywriter a 'questions and answer' routine is like a favourite old pair of shoes. We'll slip into them at the first excuse.
❍ Don't make a monkey out of yourself. People are very nice sometimes. Even the people you're going to write to. They'll do just as you say. So when, in paragraph three of your letter you casually invite them to 'take a look at the stunning new villas in this year's exciting brochure enclosed ...', they will. More often than not, most of them will look right then. Actually, it's the very last thing you want them to do. Having spent a great deal of time and effort getting them into the letter, you would much rather they continued. The trouble is they probably return to the letter. Be sure to build into copy and design the visual and verbal signposts that will help the majority of readers to get the whole story.

Guidelines for design and layout

Use layout for emphasis. Have you ever noticed how many direct mail letters use indented paragraphs? They work well to add emphasis to the importance of particular passages. I've always worked to three paragraph widths, adding shape and interest to the layout of a letter. As do indented paragraph openings. Generally the more tidied up the copy, the more boring, solid and heavy it looks – so justify left but leave 'ragged right'!

Here is my paragraph grid (not to scale!):

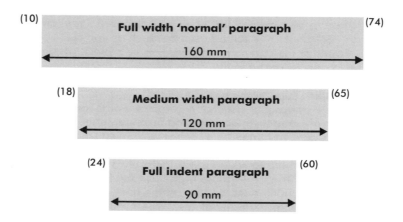

(10)   **Full width 'normal' paragraph**   (74)
160 mm

(18)   **Medium width paragraph**   (65)
120 mm

(24)   **Full indent paragraph**   (60)
90 mm

1. Minimum type size, 12 point.
2. Use a serif typeface.
3. Minimum left and right hand margins 25 mm (i.e. 10 spaces in using 10 point type).
4. Figures in brackets show spaces in from left edge.
5. Layout on 'centred' format.

TIPS

Design and layout

The functions of design in direct mail are to:
- ❑ get the words read
- ❑ enhance, illustrate, dramatise and emphasise the proposition
- ❑ illustrate, clarify and endorse the text
- ❑ show the reader the way to go, and how to deal with the various pieces
- ❑ indicate and encourage the desired response

There are other functions of design, of course, but we are essentially dealing with a very practical approach coupled with an informed and aware typographic ability – followed by how it looks, which is to many 'lay' people what they think is meant by design. A good looking piece is well designed. And an ugly piece is badly designed.

It is perfectly possible to meet the demanding requirements of the direct marketing world and satisfy the aesthetic desires of the artier aspirations of design. Direct marketing design, the more tasteful anyway, tends to settle rather more easily with a classical approach. That doesn't mean that it should be stuffy. It does mean that it should generally make looking at it a pleasant experience. It should look inviting and attractive.

To achieve our objectives, all a designer, typographer or artist has to do is think. Not about their own desires, or purposes, but about the reader's. And probably the most compromising factor of all of these is that the design should not be so striking as to distract the reader or get in the way of copy.

❝ *We don't want to hear 'What a lovely brochure'. We want to hear 'What a lovely hotel'. Or holiday. Or nest of tables. Or whatever!* ❞
German lecturer on direct mail creativity

Don't forget materials. One great way to make an impact is the vast array of different textures and weights and colours available to you. Remember my earlier advice. When they hold your mailing in their hands, they hold your company. If they don't know you, the materials – not just paper, but typography too – will be a major piece of evidence.

Designer do's and don'ts

Do ...

○ Use 'reward' psychology. Conventional advertising and marketing design operates largely on the psychology of approval. The nicer we look, the prettier we are, the more they will like us. If they like us they will admire us greatly and do as we ask. Result: 'What a lovely brochure.' Direct marketing operates more on the reward psychology, 'Hey look! If you do this, you'll get this.' It's very much more basic. In design terms it translates principally as action based formats – strong headline styles and forceful, powerful layouts. Use these while projecting your brand values and image as well as possible.

A classical designer wants to make sure something looks as nice as possible. He or she will design into the brochure (often as the last fold in an A4 concertina leaflet, for example) a reply card. To make it come together as a piece of design they have created a layout that runs across the entire spread. Perhaps a tint or illustration softened into the background. Or maybe the copy is carefully ranged around a colour pic of your building or the product range. You know the sort of thing – the design encompasses the whole spread.

This is wrong because the action you want, the card ripped off and returned, is at complete loggerheads with the designer's achievement. So the reader has to spoil or mutilate the work to do what is necessary. And to compound the felony, the better the job the designer does, the worse the conflict. The less likely it is that people will want to mutilate it or spoil it. My advice is generally to keep reply cards separate. Then nobody has to spoil anything to take the action.

Response by design

You must have seen all those leaflets and inserts where the reply card hangs off, flapping about like that cartoon of the last leaf on the autumn tree. They beg to be torn off. In fact, if the design is right, people will tear them off anyway. Even if they're not responding. Why? Because they don't look right. They look awkward and out of place. In fact, if you were just to tear that last bit off it would actually look better!

○ Make your packages readable – you would think this was obvious but design seems to go through fads or phases where small font sizes or dropping type over bright solid colours are all the rage. These simply make type harder to read. The harder something is to read the less people will bother and the less time they will give.

○ Use simple, clear typefaces, preferably serif which (apparently everybody apart from Swiss) people find easier to read. Use nothing smaller than ten point if typeset, twelve point if typewritten. I also recommend twelve point for letters. Use distinct colours for type. No fancy stuff. Don't ever make copy blend into the design.

○ Use shape and folds and construction to present the rationale for you – in copy Do's we learned to develop a rationale. In other words to orchestrate our sales story. To lead readers down a natural path of persuasion. Designers can do a fantastic job here, developing formats and paper folds so that, as the paper unfolds, so does the sales story.

○ Establish the role of each component. Think about the tasks and objectives of each individual item. Is it to inform, to entertain, to involve, to announce, to celebrate, to invite, to impress? Use design and choice of materials to make this role clear. Make the fun elements look like fun. The technical pieces look technical. Above all else, appreciate that mailings have a character; that the various components should all work together even though each may perform a different individual task.

○ Use illustration and photography to score points, not just for imagery. The sales story will benefit from illustration – photographic or otherwise – to add understanding. Remember that pictures will get looked at well in advance of the copy. Photographs generally work better than illustration. Use them carefully when and where they will add maximum emphasis to the story.

○ Use pictures with people in. People warm up print. They attract the eye. They convince. Who wants to eat in a restaurant with nobody in it? Who wants to sail on a boat that nobody else sails on? Who wants to fly on a plane that nobody else wants to fly on? Get some people power!

Answering readers' questions

Here's a useful checklist, presented component by component, of the questions that will quite naturally occur to the reader.

Envelope

○ Is this for me?
○ Who is it from? (You may choose to answer this later!)

And your existing Customers
- ○ What's it all about today?
- ○ Am I interested in this?

And cold prospects
- ○ What's in this envelope?
- ○ More important – what's in it for me?

Letter

- ○ Why are they writing to me?
- ○ What's so interesting about this? (Put your main benefit first.)
- ○ Who signed this letter?
- ○ Shall I go on reading?
- ○ Do I need this?
- ○ Again – what's in it for me? Can they prove it? Where's the evidence? What am I supposed to do?

Leaflet

- ○ How did I get along without this up to now?
- ○ Why will this make things better tomorrow?
- ○ What's in it for me? And who says so? And who can prove it?
- ○ Is it exactly what I need?
- ○ Should I react?
- ○ Is this urgent?
- ○ How do I respond?

Response device

- ○ What must I do with this? (All the way through your package you should talk about response as if it is expected.)
- ○ How easy is it? (If it is too complex or time-consuming, it will put people off.)
- ○ How much ... what's the price?
- ○ Must I sign?
- ○ What is the risk once I sign?
- ○ What happens next?
- ○ Do I have to make any decisions?
- ○ Must I fill in, or just check my details?
- ○ Must I pay postage?
- ○ Is it urgent? (Yes, yes, yes!!!)

Getting letter perfect

Letters are undoubtedly, undisputedly and consistently the single strongest weapon in the creative armoury. A good letter is a joy to read, or at the very least a pleasure. It is so formidable for a number of reasons:

People's natural instinct is to head for the letter first, often shunning more than casual glances of your other items in favour of it. This is simply the conditioning of time. We expect letters in the post. We know they'll explain what it's about. So if there's any news, or anything significant, or anything important, it'll be in there.

Letters often look the easiest to cope with, the least threatening or blatantly trying to 'sell'. Not always. But there is a comfort factor to a letter, once we've established that it's good news not bad, which we enjoy and which attracts us.

This is because letters come from people. Leaflets are issued by companies. Letters are sent by an individual. Even if they are obviously mass produced. They have signatures. They talk in a light (sometimes chatty) style. So there's obviously a person there. A person behind it. A person involved. Logically, of course, this is true of all the other items too; they just don't show it so engagingly!

Keep the momentum going. Don't do anything which might encourage the reader to quit. In fact try to do the opposite. Run-on hooks for example. That's breaking at a page end, mid sentence, mid paragraph. If possible try to build some intrigue or curiosity into the 'hook' too. Such as ...

keep your benefits too. And, of course, you could win ...

/over please

Don't number pages, unless it helps to clarify or avoid confusion – or if you are using separate pages.

Checklist for replies

The response device needs to ask for the order. It needs to close the sale. It needs to stand alone. It needs to perform its task with the minimum of fuss or effort by the responder. And lastly (meaning literally lastly – give it final priority), it needs to be economically and conveniently processed by you when it gets back. Here's a check list of ideas to help you achieve those objectives:

○ **Keep it nice and clean. Design is all important here.** Yet a lot of designers rush out the response piece, either because they get bored with it, because it's no fun designing forms, or because they think it's a fairly trivial piece of detail. Wrong. It needs to look just as attractive, logical, open and inviting as the other items. Bearing in mind all it has to do, that's often a real challenge for designers.

○ **Keep it simple** – it needs to look happy, colourful and friendly but not confusing. So use colour in the twin roles of making it cheerful and also making it easier to understand and follow.

○ **Give sufficient space** – if you can't pre-fill their name and address for them, the responder should not be forced to cramp or abbreviate their details. Nor their order or response requests. Don't lose orders for items because you didn't allow enough lines. Ask them to write in BLOCK CAPITALS.

○ **Identify it.** Ensure the response item stands out and is clearly headed. Avoid the word 'form' if you can. Slip, coupon, request, claim and application are all more positive, less formal and more inviting.

○ **Make sure they don't miss bits.** You can use emphatic arrows to highlight important bits like signatures or postal codes. Or place tinted crosses like your accountant or lawyer does in pencil to show you where to sign. You can achieve a great deal with background tints. For example, try leaving all the sections they have to fill in as white sections out of a light background. This has the added advantage of making a large piece look less than it does as a whole. You only notice the white spaces!

○ **Give clear instructions or advice** – if you have something that requires difficult, time-consuming or hard to find information, be helpful. Nothing beats a step by step guide, the 1-2-3 of 'how to apply'. If necessary give additional tips and hints alongside tricky bits. Such as '... your bank sort code is the six digit code, top right of your cheques.'

○ **Put on their name and address** – you'll boost response by filling in their basic details. Design the document so the name and address block then shows through an envelope window and you'll do yourself another favour. But find some discrete place to print a code which will also speed up your access to their record when you need to.

○ Remember the keycodes you need – the response device is the place for codes. But don't make people feel that they are just a set of numbers to you.

○ Code mailing responses for a fast handling stream. Code if you use reply envelopes for other things, or you want to apply different priorities to response handling. Code the outer envelopes or return address sides for your mail handling staff. This can be achieved by a simple change of colour. A side stripe or corner flash and so on. Or a change of department name in the address!

Talk about response as if you expect it, not as if it will surprise you! The number of times I see this ...

'If you return the reply card enclosed ...'

The very use of the word 'if' unravels almost everything you've done so far. It suggests there is another course other than response. It suggests you believe they might not want to accept your proposition. It suggests that really it might not be all that it's cracked up to be. Whereas ...

'When you return the reply paid card ...'

has an entirely different set of implications: more confident; more positive.

○ Encourage personal contact – be sure to give them a named individual to ring. And a number! You will have spent some time humanising the package, don't stop at the reply device. Print a name for them to return it to. One person sent them the letter. Let them reply to one person too. If they can be the same, that's great.

○ Tell them how to pay – make payment easy. Accept credit cards (and telephone, fax and e-mail orders!). Additionally, test 'Send no money now' if it's feasible or appropriate. Bad debt may go up. But so does response. See if one outweighs the other.

○ Go for extra or bigger sales – offer deluxe versions, or even, just as they do by the checkouts at your local store, tempt with an impulse purchase. Even if it's only gift wrapped or express delivery options. Both offer a good extra profit for you. Better still, go for real extras. You'll be surprised how this can bump up order values. And the order slip is a very hot sales area.

○ Remember their worries. Keep reassuring. This document, at one level or another, is often a commitment from them to you. So, for example, repeat the guarantee here.

○ Remember the common courtesies. Say 'thank you'. Tell them how quickly you will deliver or respond. Ask for their day/early evening phone numbers, if appropriate. And don't abuse this information.

○ Ask for further information, but not intrusively. Or, if you've already got enough, ask for the name of a friend who might also be interested, or for any forthcoming or recent address changes.

1. Readers read in three rounds: glance, scan, read.
2. There are also only three categories of reader: yes, maybe and no.
3. Use either AIDA or Bob Stone's 7 key points to build a copy structure.
4. Write what the reader wants to read *not* what the writer wants to write.
5. To write good copy simply sell the way you always have, but on paper.
6. Follow the 27 do's and don'ts to write good copy.
7. Good design gets the words read, enhances the proposition, supports the text, shows the reader what to do next, and encourages the desired response. In itself, it does not sell.
8. Letters usually get the most readership and it is always best to include one unless there is a good reason not to.
9. Reply devices are extremely important. Use the checklist above to make them effective.

What's in this chapter for you

Small business? You've got the edge
Making sure nothing goes rong!
Choosing your format

Small business? You've got the edge

Direct mail can be complicated. It involves a whole gamut of skills and many technologies: research; copywriting; graphics; photography and photographic reproduction; typesetting; printing; envelope manufacture; paper manufacturing; computer work and data processing; database or list management and broking; addressing; labelling (manual or mechanical); enclosing; postal sorting; and so on.

> ❝ *We are a family business. And we use direct mail all the time. Unlike bigger businesses, we keep it all in the family. Everything is done on the PC. We use a local printer now and again. But all the envelope folding and stuffing we do as a family sitting watching television. My fourteen year old son is the computer genius!* ❞
> **– Stephanie Parken, Designer Dress Retailer**

It's my firm belief that small businesses who often organise their own mailings are the ones who can best organise a problem-free mailing. It often has an authenticity which adds enormous power. And since it is often all handled in-house on a PC, errors don't happen. Everything is hand enclosed and checked in the process. Wonderful!

Don't be a dummy (1)!

If you are using a mailing house or 'lettershop', you need to explain how you want your mailing packed (enclosed is the word direct mailers use – occasionally it's called 'stuffing').

When sending dummies to suppliers, whether printed, made up from proofs, or 'dummied up' from photocopies of the artwork, always send two sets of each variation. Use a highlighter pen to indicate variations and notable codes. The first set should be made up as required but the envelope left unsealed, and the second set arranged to protrude about halfway out of the envelope and stapled through each corner, effectively holding everything in place.

This gives them one sample to play with and examine and another which demonstrates the precise enclosing order and pattern that you want. The stapled sample is free from some well-intentioned person trying to 'improve' your wishes or just failing to note every detail exactly as they take apart the sample to see what's what and what's how.

❝ *Never check anything! Make your standard DOUBLE-checking. Involve those who aren't involved. Get their opinions as well as their corrections.* ❞
Chris Melville, marketing manager and direct mail user

Making sure nothing goes rong!

I'm sure you have experienced the feeling of complete disbelief when somebody points at a wrong word or spelling in something you know you read and checked not once, not twice, but half a dozen times. You can't do anything about that. Your brain is picking up what it knows should be there. But others don't know. They read with a critical innocence you can never have.

The responsibility for artwork being correct always lies with the client. Not with the studio. Not with the typesetters. Not even with the agency. It's down to the client. So if there's a reprint, that's down to the client too. It's a responsibility not to be shirked, made light of or even delegated. And a responsibility that makes double-checking instead of checking well worth while. Especially check:

○ **Does the response device work, fit the return envelope and is it as easy as possible to complete?**
○ **Can recipients clearly see what they have to do to buy or enquire from you? And is it easy for them to do? Always give them plenty of room for their name, address and other details.**

- When using boxed spaces for the recipient to complete, allow a minimum of 5 mm in box depth, and ideally, 6 mm or 7 mm. A millimetre is only a small thing, but it can make a difference to the number of replies.
- Does it fit the reply envelope? You might think these little things are too silly to clutter up a book. I disagree – I've seen them all!

Try to put my name in it!

A buyer or responder needs to feel safe, relaxed and in control. That's most of what the need for simplicity and clarity is about. So the next time a studio or agency submits a reply device that gives the applicant an inch and a half to fill in their full name, the same for their company name, and then four inches for their telephone number and four more for their postal code, you know what to tell them! "I'll just see if I can write John Frazer-Robinson in that space!"

Don't be a dummy (2)!

The list of typical, silly mistakes is also the list of common mistakes. So, if I list a few, you'll probably recognise them:

- Spelling errors spotted after the job is printed
- Poor quality print through wrong or badly chosen paper and materials
- Devices that don't pop-up, appear, release or unfold correctly, because nobody made-up working dummies
- Mini-cab, bike and courier bills to cover late delivery of proofs, disks or printing plates (often due to one of the first three above)

Check the bills

This is not to check you've been charged correctly. Hopefully you'll be doing that anyway. It's to draw up a list of expenses incurred over budget – extras, corrections or errors – or things to improve quality or pull back lost time. Don't use this list as the agenda for a mud-slinging meeting with staff or suppliers. Use it as the agenda for 'How can we do it better next time?'

Talk to your postal people

Post offices around the world love direct mailers. In the UK, most of Europe, Scandinavia, Australia, New Zealand and to some extent in the USA, they have people to give you advice, helpful booklets and special rates for regular or bulk quantities.

Be aware of forthcoming price increases on paper and envelopes. Sometimes it pays to buy early. If you have standard stationery or print items which you use all the year round, try to order them at the same time as ordering items for your direct mail campaign. Volume purchasing can cut costs dramatically.

Try to make copy timeless. It's expensive to change artwork and printing plates every time you want to mail. Of course, dated material such as closing dates or special offers, and so on, are used as a device to increase response, but you should try to use them in situations where they can be changed inexpensively. Use adhesive stickers and overprints. Avoid them appearing reversed out of four colour process; one simple date change would involve four new plates.

Ensure reply envelopes or cards meet the post office regulations. The regulations are there for good reasons. Use the minimum weight and size to ensure your replies don't get trapped in other's mail or mangled in franking machines!

Choosing your format

With some occasional exceptions a 'package' should be a cohesive sales machine or enquiry generator, with each component performing a task:

○ Envelopes intrigue, lead the reader in, or introduce.
○ Letters announce. Explain. Invite. Encourage action.
○ Leaflets tell. Describe. Expand. Give detail. Illustrate and stimulate.
○ Flyers and other devices emphasise. Highlight. Carry urgent 'stop press' announcements. Provide extra fine detail. Or a last push for response.
○ Reply devices re-sell. Take orders. Encourage a dialogue. Re-illustrate offers. Reassure responders.
○ Reply envelopes bring replies, money and sensitive data.

But they all have to pull together gradually moving the reader's mind nearer to a decision – the decision to respond to your proposition.

Deciding on the format can be a difficult task. Here is a simple routine which will help you decide on number, shape, and size of your components:

- ○ What am I trying to achieve?
  - ● Why should the reader want to do it?
  - ● What will convince them?
  - ● What will make them do it now?
- ○ How can I achieve it?
  - ● What is the logic to my sales story?
  - ● What natural steps or stages does the story fall into?
  - ● How much space will I need?
- ○ Are there any practical or functional aspects relevant to the format?
  - ● Do I need to get cash back or is the reply sensitive or confidential in any way?
  - ● Is there any other reason for mailing. If so, what are the requirements (such as a bonus notice, statement, invoice, membership details, etc, etc,)? Can they be used in any way to relate or support my primary objective?
  - ● Is there anything which requires, or is worthy of, particular highlighting or emphasis?
  - ● Will the recipient need any help handling the documentation? If so, how and where should I give them that help and advice?
- ○ Which of the options open to me:
  - ● will make the most sense to them if handled as I want, but will still work if dropped, misunderstood or mis-handled by the reader?
  - ● will work hardest to dramatise the sales story and be interesting for the reader?
  - ● will work out best from production, timing and budget points of view?

And then to review your decision:

- ○ As a cohesive selling machine:
  - ● does it work?
  - ● is it logical, clear, and simple to assimilate?
- ○ Is there anything I can do to improve it, make it more interesting, useful, or simple to handle and respond to?

Remember: it is quite possible that, in achieving as many as possible of the above you may fall upon a pretty basic format. There is nothing wrong with that. You can still use materials – paper, texture, and three-dimensional objects to add an extra lift!

1. Use all the checklists in this chapter to save you time, heartache and money.
2. Involve others in your checking process – get their opinions and ideas as well as their corrections.
3. Choose your format carefully. Remember each component has a role but they all have to work together. Each piece of print should include your proposition or offer. And your contact information – a phone number at least.

If you check out some of the other books I'm writing in this special series – *Building Customer Loyalty*, *High Performance Sales Management*, *Writing Great Sales Letters* – you'll find your direct mail skills will be even more useful to you than you might appreciate right now.

And if you have a website or regularly send e-mail, the copy and design advice applies equally to electronic or computerised communications. In direct mail, the creative element has always been my first love: finding the big idea; writing the copy; directing the design. Therefore in writing this tailpiece, I would dearly love to point you in the direction of creative things as being the most important but …

One last secret!

Before you do anything else, concentrate on getting your lists and other data in the best possible shape. Lists and targeting are vital to success. Start to learn as much as possible about your Customers and prospects; not as names on a database but as the individuals they are. This knowledge yields all the potential answers to your questions of timing, the offer or proposition (or both) and, of course, the creative approach. And the last secret for you is that, if you put targeting at the top of that list, this is not only the best order in which to tackle things, but also my recommended priorities as far as investment of both your time and money are concerned.

Go for it!